LIVING IN
AFRICA

Living in
SOUTH AFRICA

Jen Green

W
FRANKLIN WATTS
LONDON•SYDNEY

Franklin Watts
First published in Great Britain in 2016 by The Watts Publishing Group

Credits
Series Editor: Julia Bird
Editor: Sarah Silver
Series Design: D.R. ink

ISBN 978 1 4451 4868 7

Picture credits: Africa Media Online/Alamy: 14t. Air Images/Shutterstock: 17t. Wolf Avni/Shutterstock: 12b. Roger Bamber/Alamy: 17b. Heinrich van den Berg/Gallo/Alamy: 20t. RosaIreneBetancourt5/Alamy: 10t. RosaIreneBetancourt10/Alamy: 8t bikeriderlondon/Shutterstock: 12t, 18t. Birdiegal/Shutterstock: 13t. Lenise Calleja/Dreamstime: 15b. Dominique de La Croix/Shutterstock: 5b. Damian322/Dreamstime: 5t. Demerzel21/Dreamstime: 9b. EcoPrint/Shutterstock: 16b. EPA/Alamy: 20b, 21t. EPA/Jon Hrusa/Alamy: 16c. Everett Historical/Shutterstock: 8b. Inna Felker/Shutterstock: 13b, 19t. Therina Groenewald/Shutterstock: 19c. Robert Harding PL/Superstock: 4t. imagebroker/Superstock: 13c. Alexander Joe/AFP/Getty Images: 14b. michael jung/Shutterstock: 19b, 23. Keystone/Getty Images: 7t. Daleen Loest/Shutterstock: 8br. Benny Marty/Shutterstock: 6t. Mayabuns/Shutterstock: 11t. Media24/Gallo/Getty Images: 21b. Micoppiens/Dreamstime: 14c. Denis Mironov/Shutterstock: front cover. Juan Nel/Dreamstime: 11b. Per-Anders Pettersson/Getty Images: 6b. Raymond Preston/Sunday Times/Gallo/Getty Images: 7b. Mari Swanepoel/Shutterstock: 18b. Cedric Weber/Shutterstock: 10b. Andrea Wilmore/Dreamstime: 9t. Anke van Wyk/Shutterstock: 15t. Ariadne Van Zandbergen/Alamy: 16t.

Printed in China

MIX
Paper from
responsible sources
FSC® C104740
FSC
www.fsc.org

Franklin Watts
An imprint of
Hachette Children's Group
Part of The Watts Publishing Group
Carmelite House
50 Victoria Embankment
London EC4Y 0DZ

An Hachette UK Company
www.hachette.co.uk

www.franklinwatts.co.uk

Contents

Words in bold are in the glossary on page 23.

Welcome to South Africa

Hi! I come from South Africa.

Where is South Africa?

South Africa is the size of France and Spain put together. It lies at the southern tip of Africa. The ocean surrounds it on three sides. Namibia, Botswana, Zimbabwe, Swaziland and Mozambique lie on the northern **border.** The small country of Lesotho lies inside South Africa.

The Kalahari Desert is in the north of South Africa.

Landscapes

South Africa is a beautiful country with many different **landscapes**. There are craggy mountains, rolling grasslands, thorny woods, and deserts with mile after mile of burning sand.

What's the weather like?

South Africa has a mild **climate.** The weather is usually warm and sunny. The west is very dry. The east **coast** is wetter and greener. South Africa lies in the southern half of the world, so seasons fall at the opposite times to Europe and North America. From December to February it is summer. Winter lasts from June to August.

The green east coast

People of South Africa

South Africa is home to many different peoples — not just black Africans like me, but also Europeans and Asians. It is sometimes called the rainbow nation because people from many different places live here.

Mix of people

Black Africans were the first people of South Africa. Europeans, such as Dutch and English settlers, arrived from the 1600s. In the 1800s people from India and Malaysia came to work here. All of these groups speak different languages and have different **customs** and beliefs.

White rule

In the 1900s South Africa was ruled by white people. Whites and non-whites lived separately – this system was called **apartheid**. Black people and other non-whites were treated unfairly, and were not allowed to vote for the country's government.

Only white people could go on this beach.

Freedom

Many people worked to end this unfair system. In 1994 all adult South Africans were allowed to vote for the first time. People queued for hours to vote!

People queuing to vote in the 1994 elections.

Cities

Most South Africans live in towns and cities. The largest cities are Johannesburg, Cape Town, Durban and Pretoria. We live in Cape Town, on the south coast.

Mining town

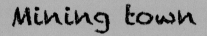

Many people moved to Johannesburg when gold was discovered there in the 1880s. Now it is the biggest city. South Africa is rich in **minerals**, including gold and diamonds. It has some of the world's deepest mines.

Some of the world's biggest diamonds were found in South Africa. This giant hole was once a diamond mine.

Table Mountain

Cape Town

Cape Town is a beautiful city on the south coast. Nearby is a famous flat-topped mountain called Table Mountain. You can ride a cable car to the top to get a great view of the city.

Government buildings in Pretoria

Three capitals

South Africa has three **capital** cities. Cape Town is the home of Parliament. The government meets here to make laws. The government departments are based in Pretoria. The main law courts are in Bloemfontein.

Town and country

*Most rich people in South Africa live near city centres. Poorer people live in the country or on the outskirts of cities. We live outside Johannesburg in a **township** called Soweto.*

Townships

Townships are poor districts on the edge of cities. Soweto is a big township. It's crowded but friendly. Children play games on the streets and the houses are quite small. My brother and I sleep together in the same bed!

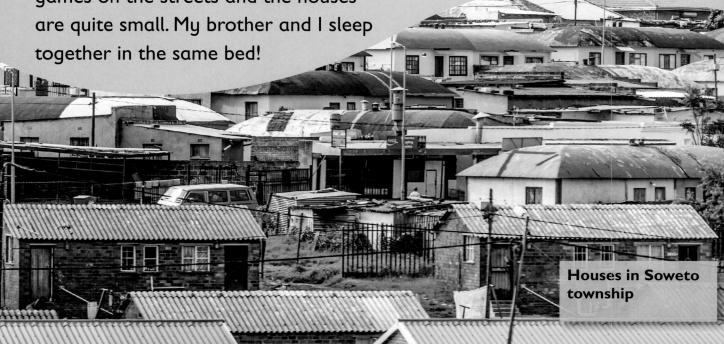

Houses in Soweto township

Country life

Most people in the countryside work as farmers. Village homes are small. Often there is no water or electricity, so people fetch water from the river or a well.

Some village houses are round with thatched roofs.

Moving to the city

Many country people move to the cities to find work, but homes and jobs are hard to find in cities too. Some people live in shacks made of scrap wood and metal. These areas on the outskirts of cities are called **shanty towns**.

shanty town

Scenery and wildlife

South Africa has many kinds of scenery. In different areas you can see rocky mountains, forests, grasslands, scorching deserts and sandy beaches. Each of these places has its own plants and animals.

Mountains and deserts

Much of South Africa is a high, flattish land called a **plateau**. The Drakensberg mountain range in the east is snow-covered in winter. The Kalahari Desert in the north-west is very dry.

The Drakensberg mountain range

Savannah wildlife

Dry grasslands called the **savannah** cover much of the plateau. They are home to amazing animals, including lions, cheetahs, giraffes and elephants. Herds of antelope and zebra wander in search of fresh grass.

Penguins on the south-west coast

South Africa is home to the three biggest land animals: elephants, hippos (above) and rhinos. You can also see the tallest animal, the giraffe, and the biggest bird, the ostrich.

Coasts

South African coasts are washed by the Atlantic and Pacific oceans. Whales swim in these waters, while seals and penguins live on the coast.

What we eat

Maize (corn), rice and beans are the main foods eaten in South Africa. My favourite dish is chicken soup!

Mealies

Cornmeal, which we call mealies, is the main food for most families. At school we eat porridge called *pap* for breakfast. We also eat mealies at lunch and dinner, with vegetables or a meat stew for a treat.

Try koeksisters for a sweet treat — these are plaited doughnuts soaked in syrup.

Barbecues

Rich people eat more meat. Outdoor barbecues called *braii* are popular in summer. Spicy sausages and kebabs sizzle on the barbecue. Dried strips of meat, called *biltong*, make a tasty snack.

bobotie

Eastern flavours

Indian and Malay people brought their own styles of cooking to South Africa. Asian dishes include curries and sweet and sour sauces. *Bobotie* is a dish from Malaysia. Minced lamb or beef is baked with curry spices and served with yellow rice.

Having fun

Sunny South Africa is a great place to spend time outdoors. We love sport and other outdoor fun.

Sport

Football is the most popular sport. In 2010 South Africa hosted the Football World Cup. Rugby, cricket, tennis, boxing and athletics are also popular. The national rugby side, the Springboks, won the Rugby World Cup in 1995 and 2007.

The Springboks playing against Wales

The springbok, a fast-running antelope, is a symbol of South Africa.

Outdoor activities

In summer people head to the coast for swimming, surfing and sailing. You can go out in a boat to spot whales, dolphins or even a great white shark! Or you can head for the mountains to go hiking, horse riding and mountain biking.

Music

South Africans love music, singing and dancing. You can hear many different styles, including jazz, **rap, hip-hop, gospel,** and **traditional** African drumming. South Africa is famous for its youth choirs. Many church services include singing, clapping and dancing.

Famous places

South Africa has many fantastic places to visit. Wildlife is a big attraction – our country has the greatest wildlife show on Earth!

Wildlife

Parks and **reserves** are great places to see wildlife. At Kruger National Park you can see lions, elephants, leopards, rhinos and buffalos. These animals are known as the 'big five'.

White rhinos in Kruger National Park

Fish and flowers

Cape Town has a brilliant aquarium called the Two Oceans Aquarium. You can see sharks, seals, penguins and bright tropical fish. The area around Cape Town is famous for its flowers, many of which are found only in South Africa.

South Africa's national flower is the king protea. These unusual flowers grow up to 30 cm across.

Creepy caves

Cango Caves are amazing caves with **stalactites** and **stalagmites**. These are like stone icicles rising from the floor and hanging from the ceiling. They are formed by dripping water.

Festivals and holidays

Most South Africans are Christians, like us. There are also Muslims, Hindus and Jews. Some people follow traditional African religions.

Festivals

For Christians the main holidays are Christmas and Easter. In South Africa Christmas comes in mid-summer! Easter Monday is Family Day. Hindus, Muslims, Jews and followers of African religions have their own festivals. A group of South Africans called Zulus celebrate Shaka Day. Shaka was a great warrior who founded the Zulu nation.

A Christian church service

Celebrating freedom

National holidays mark important days in the country's history. Freedom Day celebrates the 1994 election — the first in which all adult South Africans could vote.

Nelson Mandela

People also celebrate Mandela Day. Nelson Mandela led the movement to end apartheid. The white government arrested him. He spent 27 years in prison, mostly on an island off Cape Town. He was freed in 1990. In 1994 he became South Africa's first black president.

South Africa: Fast facts

Capital: South Africa has three capitals: Cape Town, Pretoria and Bloemfontein.

Population: 53 million (2013)

Area: 1.2 million sq km

Official languages: Afrikaans, English, Ndebele, Northern Sotho, Sesotho, Swati, Tsonga, Tswana, Venda, Xhosa and Zulu.

Currency: The rand

Main religions: Christianity, Islam, Judaism, Hinduism, traditional African religions

Longest river: Orange River, 2,220 km

Highest mountain: Mafadi, 3,450 m

National holidays: New Year's Day (1 January), Human Rights Day (21 March), Good Friday, Family Day, Freedom Day (27 April), Workers Day (1 May), Youth Day (16 June), National Women's Day (9 August), Heritage Day (24 September), Day of Reconciliation (16 December), Christmas Day (25 December), Day of Goodwill (26 December)

Glossary

apartheid the official policy in South Africa that kept people of different races apart

border the boundary that divides two countries

capital usually the main city where the country's government meets; in South Africa government power is split between three capital cities

climate the regular weather pattern in a region

coast where the land meets the sea

cornmeal meal made from ground maize (corn), known in South Africa as mealies

customs a traditional way of doing things that has been followed for many years

gospel a style of Christian music

hip-hop a style of music featuring rap

landscape the natural scenery

minerals solid, non-living substances of which the Earth is made

pap porridge made from cornmeal

plateau a flat-topped area of high ground

rap popular music with a strong rhythm and spoken words

reserve a protected area of land

savannah tropical grassland

shanty town group of makeshift homes made from scrap metal, wood and cardboard

stalactite an icicle-like stone structure hanging from a cave roof, formed by dripping water

stalagmite a stone column rising from a cave floor, formed by dripping water

township a poor district on the edge of a city in South Africa, traditionally home to black people

traditional something that has been done in the same way for many years

Index

A

apartheid 7, 21

B

Bloemfontein 4, 9, 22
borders 4

C

Cango Caves 19
Cape Town 4, 8, 9, 19, 21, 22
cities 8–11
climate 5
coast 5, 8, 9, 12, 13, 17
countryside 10, 11

D

Drakensberg 4, 12

E

elections 7, 21

F

festivals 20–21, 22
flowers 19
food 14–15
Freedom Day 21, 22

H

holidays 20–21, 22

J

Johannesburg 4, 8, 10

K

Kalahari Desert 4, 5, 12

L

landscapes 5, 12–13
languages 6, 22

M

Mandela, Nelson 21
mining 8
mountains 4, 5, 9, 12, 17, 22
music 17

P

peoples 6–7
population 22
Pretoria 4, 8, 9, 22

R

religions 20, 22

S

Shaka 20
shanty towns 11
sport 16–17

T

Table Mountain 9
townships 10

W

weather 5
wildlife 12–13, 16, 17, 18–19